Contents

CW00385163

Birdwatching
Linnet .....
Crossbill ...
Ring Ouzel .
Red Kite ....
Wheatear ...
Stonechat ... . IU
Whinchat 11
Dartford Warbler 12
Hen Harrier 13
Quick ticklist 14-15
Raven 16
Nightjar 17
Hobby 18
Woodlark 19
Red Grouse 20
Curlew 21
Golden Plover 22
Redstart 23
Skylark 24
Goldcrest 25
Great Grey Shrike 26
Buzzard 27
Lapwing 28
More birds 29
Notes & Sketches 30-31
Index 32

HILL & HEATHLAND BIRDS

A Birdwatching Logbook

Birdwatching Tips

The aim of this series is to encourage you to look out for the birds around you, and record when and where you see them.

It is important to get to know how a bird moves, flies, and sings as well as identifying the shape, so the illustrations are there to show you important features to look out for, and the accompanying text tells you how the bird behaves.

Becoming familiar with common birds allows you to spot rarer sightings, so this book is to help you practise your birdcraft and enable you to become acquainted with the birds in your area and beyond.

Carduelis cannabina

Body length: *12-14cm*

Where to spot:

Gorse bushes, scrubby

hedges, grassland

Resident

LINNET

The coral-pink breast and forehead of the male Linnet are a lovely sight when the sun shines on them, especially coupled with their favourite perch: bright yellow gorse. They breed in scrubby areas and thick bushes, but also gardens near the coast. Females are a streaky brown, as are the juveniles. Linnets feed on seeds and insects, and flit up and down catching small flies, or tease seeds from the wild flowers that proliferate on the chalk grassland.

Their song is melodious and pretty - so much so that they used to be kept as a songbird.

Date	Notes

CROSSBILL

Loxia curvirostra

Body length: *15-17cm*

Where to spot:

High up in coniferous

trees

Resident

These chunky finches, as the name suggests, have the most incredible beaks with crossed mandibles. This remarkable adaptation enables seeds to be teased from larch, spruce, and pine cones.

The male is a bright tomato-red, and the female is a khaki-green. They feed high up in the canopy, and tend to keep quiet as they do so, making them quite a tricky bird to spot.

Crossbills have a metallic "kipp-kipp-kipp!" which, with the discarded conifer cones, is a sign of their whereabouts.

Date	Notes

Turdus torquatus

Body length: *24-27cm*

Where to spot:

Uplands, scrubby areas,

rocky slopes

Summer visitor

Ring Ouzels are close relatives of our more familiar garden Blackbirds, and there is a marked resemblance, although the migratory Ring Ouzels are more streamlined than their sedentary cousins, and of course sport a smart white collar, although the females have more muted colouring.

They breed on hills and high ground, using heather to make their cup-shaped nests during the summer months, before heading south to warmer areas to overwinter.

Their call is a sharp "chik!", and their song is a rather repetitive and melancholy series of notes.

Date	Notes

RED KITE

Milvus milvus

Body length: 61-72cm

Where to spot:

Cruising over hills and woodland

Resident

These large and rangy birds of prey were saved from extinction thanks to reintroduction in the 1980s to various parts of the country. They are now commonly seen in many areas flying over hills, easily recognised by their forked tail and dark-tipped angled wings in flight. If the lighting is favourable you can see their beautiful fox-red plumage. They eat mainly carrion but will also take small mammals.

For a large bird they have quite a puny call: a rather thin and piping "wee-ooooo weeee-oooo".

Date	Notes

Oenanthe oenanthe

Body length: *14-16cm*

Where to spot:

Gorse scrub, rocky

outcrops

Summer visitor

The upright stance of this pretty bird indicates it is a member of the thrush family. Wheatears visit our country during the summer having wintered in Africa, and their breeding grounds are on higher ground and heathland. In flight, the white tail with black T-bar is very distinctive as they flit between their insect hunting grounds.

Females are more creamy and rufous in their colouring, and lack the striking black eye mask of the males.

A Wheatear's song is a short, buzzy ditty.

Date	Notes

STONECHAT

Saxicola rubicola

Body length: *11-13cm*

Where to spot:

Heathland areas, scrub and gorse

Resident

This Robin-sized bird often lives in windswept areas with gorse and tussocky grass where it both nests and hunts for its main food: insects.

The male has a characteristic habit of perching atop a tall stem where his smart white collar, black head and russet-gold breast show to best effect; the female has less dramatic markings.

They have a sharp "tack" of alarm (a little like stones being knocked together, hence the name) as well as a more melodious song with a slightly scratchy quality.

Date	Notes

Saxicola rubetra

Body length: *12-14cm*

Where to spot:

Rough pasture, tussocky

grassland, wet meadows

Summer visitor

WHINCHAT

These pretty chats are a treat to see when they visit our shores from their wintering grounds in Africa. They are a stripy version of their Stonechat cousins. Whinchats are so named after the gorse or 'whin' where they like to nest and perch.

Males and females of all ages have a pale supercilium (eyebrow) although a mature male's is bright white rather than the creamy-buff of a female or juvenile.

Their call is a series of buzzy notes, interspersed with tuneful whistles.

Date	Notes

Sylvia undata

Body length: *13-14cm*

Where to spot:

Heathland, gorse, coastal

scrub and bushes

Resident

These cheery little warblers love gorse and heather, so heath and coniferous woodland are the preferred habitat. They have a wine-red chest (less vibrant on the female) and a grey head, and the males with their slight crest can be seen perched atop a gorse bush, tail raised. They nest low to the ground, but the choice of prickly shrub helps protect them from predators.

Their song is warbler-ish: a little bit scratchy and not particularly musical: "diddle-ee-diddle-eee-dee-dee" with other whistling and buzzing notes at a fast tempo.

Date	Notes

Circus cyaneus

Body length: *45-55cm*

Where to spot:

Heather moors, upland

marshes

Resident

HEN HARRIER

Hen Harriers are among the most persecuted birds of prey, with their predilection for hens - or these days, grouse - meaning they are in constant conflict with humans. Effective predators, they glide over the moor, pouncing on small mammals and birds, and pass food to each other during courtship. The males are light grey with a white rump and pale underparts, the black wing tips being a feature. Females are mottled brown with a white rump.

They have a rather reedy voice, as well as sounding out a chattering contact or alarm call.

Date	Notes

Use this page as a quick ticklist

Date completed:

RAVEN

Corvus corax

Body length: *54-67cm*

Where to spot:

Heathland, rocky upland

areas

Resident

Ravens are our largest corvid, and they nest on and around cliffs and high ground. Noticeably bigger than the more familiar Carrion Crow, Ravens have a heavy beak with a feathery base. They eat carrion, insects, small mammals, and will also take eggs and chicks.

Ravens pair for life, and build an inaccessible nest out of sticks in tall trees.

Their call is deep and loud: "krorrr korrrr" and easily recognisable.

Date	Notes

Caprimulgus europaeus

Body length: *24-28cm*

Where to spot:

Pine woodland,

heathlands

Summer visitor

NIGHTJAR

These astonishing birds winter in Africa and visit our shores to take advantage of our (sadly declining) moth and beetle population; they are night feeders. With a huge gaping mouth, they flit through the evening sky catching insects, using their large eyes to spot them.

During the day they sit on a branch, their mottled brown plumage blending so well with the bark they are almost impossible to spot. Their nest is a simple scrape on the ground.

The rolling, churring call is unique: they can sing for hours.

Date	Notes

Falco subbuteo

Body length: *29-35cm*

Where to spot:

Heaths, woodland

edges

Summer visitor

These falcons visit us in summer, and are voracious and skilled predators, taking tricksy prey like dragonflies and swallows, performing aerial swoops and stoops to catch, kill, and eat on the wing. Heathlands are a great place for insects and small birds, so Hobbys are not an uncommon sight. They have rusty-red 'trousers' and a streaky belly making them a distinctive raptor.

The most likely call to hear is the insistent "kyew kyew kyew" which varies in tempo.

Date	Notes

Lullula arborea

Body length: *13-15cm*

Where to spot:

Pine copses, open heath

with some trees

Resident

WOODLARK

These larks are short and stubby, with rounded wings and an undulating flight. Their pale eyestripe is noticeable, and they tend to perch at the top of shrubs to deliver their song, differing from the more aerial Skylark. They have a well-defined crown and a little chequerboard on the wing.

They breed in heathland areas in southern and eastern England, with some birds migrating to the continent for the winter as they don't thrive in severe cold.

They have a lovely song, full of chirrups and tuneful notes.

Date	Notes

RED GROUSE

Lagopus lagopus scotica

Body length: *33-38cm*

Where to spot:

Heather moors and

uplands

Resident

Red Grouse are well-known gamebirds, living all year round in their moorland home. They eat heather shoots, berries, and insects which sustain them in this rather harsh habitat.

Beautifully camouflaged in russet browns, with feathery legs and a bright red wattle over the eye. Sexes look the same, but the males perform a dramatic display flight, springing straight up and then gliding down.

The call is a series of nasal barks.

Date	Notes

Numenius arquata

Body length: *48-57cm*

Where to spot:

Open boggy areas,

heather moorland

Resident

CURLEW

Windswept moors and uplands are the perfect spot for Curlews during the summer breeding season, travelling to the coast to feed, probing the sand and mud for worms and crustaceans.

The long curved beak (up to 15cm on females) is probably the Curlew's most distinctive feature; the beautiful black diamonds in the ochre feathers only visible when spied through binoculars.

The name Curlew is onomatopoeic: an evocative "cour-lii" echoing across the landscape.

Date	Notes

21

Pluvialis apricaria

Body length: *25-28cm*

Where to spot:

Boggy moors, mountains,

upland pasture

Resident

These gorgeous plovers breed on our mountainsides and moorlands, migrating up and down the country and across Europe between their summer and winter grounds like many of our 'resident' species. Winter plumage is less contrasty; more of a speckled ochre but still beautiful.

The nest is a simple scrape in the heather, and they eat berries, worms, insects and seeds, preferring drier ground compared with other waders.

Golden Plovers have a slightly tooting "pee-oooo pyooo" call.

Date	Notes

Phoenicurus phoenicurus

Body length: *13-14cm*

Where to spot:

Pine forest, stone walls,

wooded hills

Summer visitor

The bright orange-red of the Redstart's tail is what gives this handsome bird its name; *steort* is Anglo-Saxon for 'tail'. Males and females sport this bright plumage, although only the male has the black face and white forehead. They seem proud of their tails, as they flick and splay the feathers during courtship.

Visiting from Africa, Redstarts build nests in a suitable crevice, and rear their young before heading south; they can frequently be seen on passage.

Their song is a gentle whistle followed by "tic! tic! tic!".

Date	Notes

SKYLARK

Alauda arvensis

Body length: *16-18cm*

Where to spot:

High above vegetated

areas, fenceposts

Resident

Despite a rather nondescript appearance, the Skylark is one of our most accomplished songsters, showing fitness and vigour to predators, potential mates and rivals by performing its song while flying upwards with fluttering wings.

They have streaks of black in the tawny plumage, with white feathers on the outer edges of the tail.

A Skylark's song is a marathon of trills, whistles, chirrups and mimicry, lasting up to 15 minutes, and from a height of 100 metres or more.

Date	Notes

Regulus regulus

Body length: *8-9cm*

Where to spot:

Woodland, heathland,

dense shrubbery

Resident

GOLDCREST

Our smallest bird the Goldcrest is really tiny, and makes itself even more difficult to spot because it loves dense shrubbery. This illustration is of a female, as she has no orange on her crest; the male has a burnished tip to the gold crown, but both sexes are distinctive as they weave through the undergrowth or up in the canopy. They eat small insects and spiders.

Their call is a very high-pitched "zweee-zweee-zweee", and their song, a similarly reedy, piccolo-esque ditty.

Date	Notes

GREAT GREY SHRIKE

Lanius excubitor

Body length: *21-26cm*

Where to spot:

Perched on fenceposts,

open heathland

Winter visitor

The shrike family, of which the Great Grey is the largest we have visiting our shores, has a rather macabre lifestyle, chasing and hunting small birds and mammals which it impales on thorny twigs or barbed wire for eating later.

Sitting on a favoured perch in upland woods, this sporadic winter visitor can be spotted by its pale undersides against the low sun as it looks out for potential prey.

The black eye mask gives a suitably bandit-like look.

It is unlikely to be heard outside the breeding season.

Date	Notes

Buteo buteo

Body length: *48-56cm*

Where to spot:

Large trees, hilly areas,

soaring overhead

Resident

BUZZARD

Buzzards are often seen soaring on the currents of warm air that rise over the fields and woods and in flight, and hold their wings in a characteristic shallow 'v' shape. Their plumage is variable from dark brown to almost white.

They eat carrion as well as worms, beetles, and small mammals, and can be seen strutting over fields in a rather ungainly manner looking for food.

They are very vocal birds, and have a piercing "peee-ayy" call when flying or perching.

Date	Notes

27

Vanellus vanellus

Body length: *28-31cm*

Where to spot:

Arable fields, pasture, wet meadows

Resident

Lapwings are large plovers, with a distinctive crest and wide, rounded black wings with white tips. Often flying in large groups in formation, their slow, flappy flight is also distinctive. The males perform an impressive tumbling flight in spring to woo the females.

Being ground-nesting birds like the Curlew and Golden Plover, they are hampered by disturbance during the breeding season causing numbers to decline.

The other name for a lapwing is a peewit, so named for the flight call of "peee-wit!"; their actual song is more musical.

Date	Notes

More birds you may see:

REED BUNTING

GREEN WOODPECKER

SHORT-EARED OWL

PEREGRINE FALCON

WHITETHROAT

*You will find
these in the
other books
in the series*

Notes & Sketches